RAIN FOREST ANIMALS
QUESTIONS & ANSWERS

MICHAEL CHINERY

ILLUSTRATED BY DAVID HOLMES
AND BERNARD ROBINSON

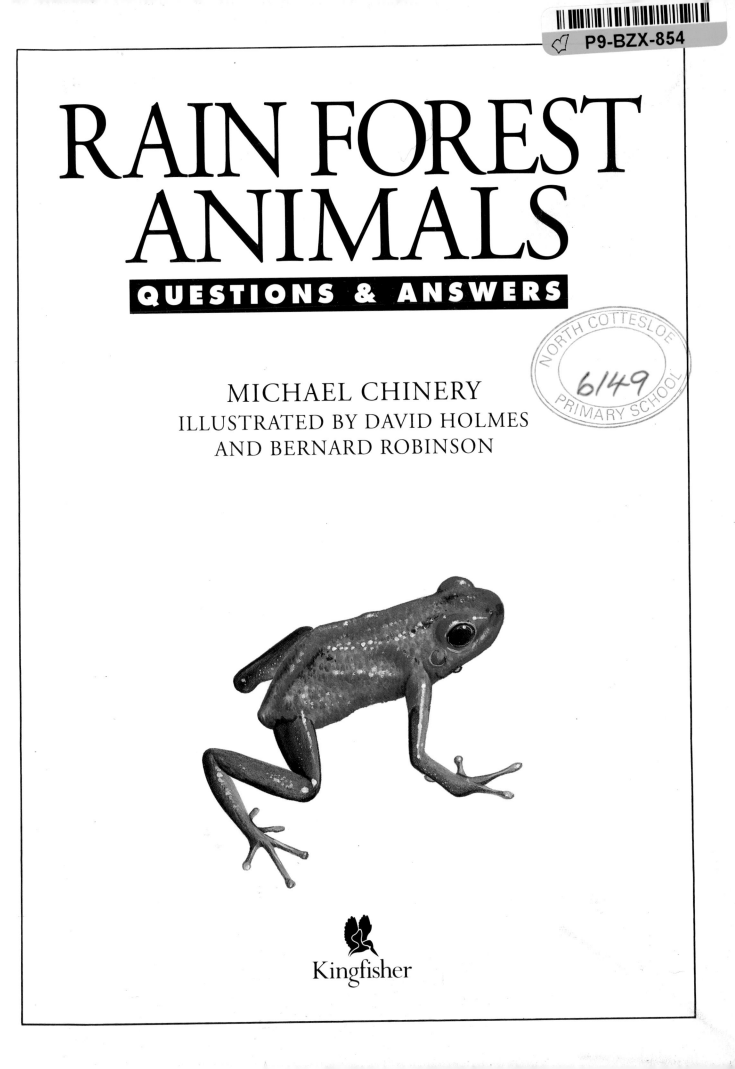

Kingfisher

KINGFISHER
An imprint of Larousse plc
Elsley House, 24–30 Great Titchfield Street,
London W1P 7AD

This edition published by Kingfisher 1995

10 9 8 7 6 5 4 3 2 1

Copyright © Larousse plc 1995

Originally published by Kingfisher 1991 in the
Wild World of Animals series
Copyright © Grisewood & Dempsey Ltd 1991

A CIP catalogue record for this book is available from the
British Library

ISBN 1 85697 305 0

Series editor: Mike Halson
Series designer: Terry Woodley
Designer: David West Children's Books
Cover design: Ian Butterworth
Illustrators: David Holmes (1, 2–5, 8–9, 10 bottom, 11,
20–21, 24–27, 32–35, 38); Ray Hutchins (10 top);
Bernard Robinson (6–7, 12–19, 22–23, 28–31, 36–37)
Cover illustration: John Butler

Phototypeset by Southern Positives and Negatives
(SPAN), Lingfield, Surrey.
Printed and bound in Hong Kong

CONTENTS

WHERE DO RAIN FORESTS GROW?

Rain forests grow in places where there is lots of rain. Most rain forests are found in the tropics, on either side of the Equator. Most of the plants there are evergreen – they never drop all their leaves at once, but grow the whole year round in the hot, steamy atmosphere. Animals live at all levels in the forest, from the ground to the tree-tops.

RAIN FOREST FACTS

● About 50 hectares of tropical rain forest are cut down every minute – that's an area of more than 100 football pitches.

● The tallest trees in the tropical rain forest are 50 metres high.

DO YOU KNOW

Some rain forests are huge, but altogether they still only cover about one-twentieth of the Earth's surface. Even so, scientists believe that the rain forests contain more than half of the world's plant and animal species.

TROPICAL RAIN FORESTS

Tropical rain forests are found around the world in areas near the Equator. For this reason they are sometimes called equatorial rain forests. The three main tropical rain forest regions are around the River Amazon in South America, in central Africa, and in Indonesia. Over half of the world's rain forests are found in South America.

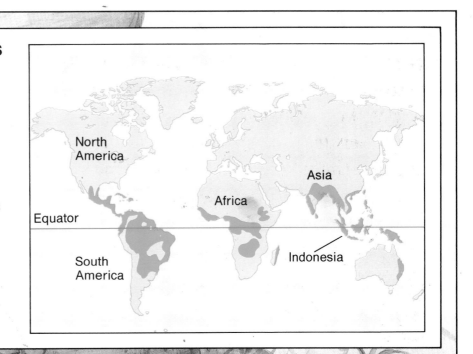

WHICH ANIMALS ARE GENTLE GIANTS?

Gorillas are the largest of the apes. People once thought they were fierce and dangerous, but they are really quite gentle and friendly creatures. They roam through the African rain forest in small groups and feed almost entirely on leaves. Each group is ruled by an old male. He decides where the group will feed each day.

GORILLA FACTS

● Large male gorillas are nearly 2 metres tall and weigh 200 kg.

● Gorillas may live for up to 37 years.

The group leader is always an old male with silvery hair on his back. He is called a silverback.

Gorillas have superb eyesight and the leader keeps a watchful eye on the whole group.

Male gorillas thump their chests when they are angry, or just to show off their great strength.

Gorillas like to sit together in the middle of the day. Females spend a lot of time grooming their babies.

SURVIVAL WATCH

Gorillas are big animals and they have nothing to fear from other wild animals. People are their main problem. We keep cutting down the forests, and if this goes on much longer the gorillas will have nowhere to live. The World Wide Fund for Nature and other organisations are working hard to save the gorillas. They are raising money to create special reserves where the animals can live in safety.

DO YOU KNOW

Gorillas make cosy beds every night with leafy branches. Females often sleep in the trees, but big males have to make their beds down on the ground.

WHERE DO LEMURS LIVE?

The lemurs are distant cousins of the monkeys. There are 22 different kinds and they live only on the African island of Madagascar. They have survived there for millions of years because there have never been any real monkeys on the island to compete with them. Most lemurs roam the forests in small groups. Some are active at night, but most of them feed in the daytime. They eat fruit, leaves, bark and insects.

Ring-tailed lemurs are the only lemurs that spend much time on the ground. They live in groups of up to 30 animals.

THE BOUNCING INDRI

The indri is the biggest lemur. It is over 1 metre long, but has only a tiny tail. It makes spectacular leaps through the trees. On the ground it bounces along on its big back legs.

 SURVIVAL WATCH

Lemurs are much less common than they were 100 years ago. Some are in real danger of extinction because the forests of Madagascar are being destroyed. But recently people have realized that the lemurs are great tourist attractions, and special reserves are being set up for them.

● Most lemurs are cat-sized or squirrel-sized. Mouse lemurs are the smallest type. Their bodies are only 12 cm long and they weigh only about 60 grams.

The tail of the ring-tailed lemur is up to 60 cm long and is used to signal to other groups of lemurs that the area is occupied.

THE NOCTURNAL AYE-AYE

The cat-sized aye-aye is a strange and very rare lemur. Its big eyes and ears show that it is a nocturnal creature – it comes out at night. It hooks insects from tree trunks with its wire-like middle finger. The aye-aye also uses this slender finger to comb its fur. During the day, the aye-aye spends its time in a hollow tree or among branches.

WHICH INSECT PRETENDS TO BE A FLOWER?

The devil's flower is a kind of African mantis, and it is a living trap for other insects. The insects think they are visiting a flower, until the mantis grabs them with its spiky legs.

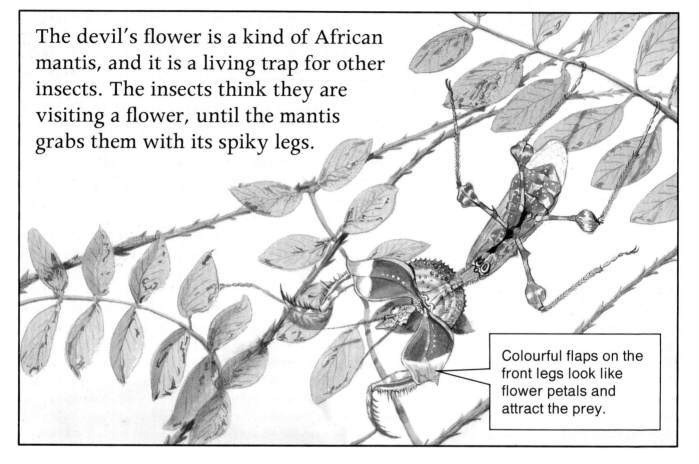

Colourful flaps on the front legs look like flower petals and attract the prey.

WHICH MONKEY GOES RED IN THE FACE?

Mandrills are ground-living monkeys from the forests of Central Africa. The red on the male's face gets brighter if he becomes angry.

MANDRILL FACTS

● Mandrills live in family groups and talk to each other with grunts. They sleep in the trees.

● Females and young are not as brightly coloured as the males.

A mandrill walks on its hands and feet. Its long fingers are useful for gathering food and carrying it to its mouth.

Why does the colobus monkey look fat?

Colobus monkeys live in Africa and feed only on leaves. They have to eat lots of leaves to get enough nourishment, so they have big stomachs and always look fat. They sit around more than other monkeys because they need more time to digest their food.

The colobus has no thumbs. Its hands simply hook over the branches as it swings through the trees.

The tail cannot curl around branches like the tails of American monkeys (see page 18).

How do tarsiers hunt?

Tarsiers are little relatives of the monkeys. They feed on all sorts of small animals, which they find with their sharp eyes and ears. They leap on to their prey and kill it with their teeth.

 SURVIVAL WATCH

Tarsiers live in the forests of South-East Asia. They are quite common in some places, but their numbers are falling fast as the forests are being destroyed.

Big eyes enable the tarsier to see well at night. Big ears also give the animal excellent hearing.

WHERE DO CHIMPANZEES LIVE?

Chimpanzees are apes and they are our closest relatives among the wild animals. They live in the forests of Africa and feed mainly on fruit. People once thought that chimps fed entirely on plants, but they eat quite a lot of meat as well. They often kill pigs and antelope. Male chimps sometimes work in teams to trap monkeys in the trees. If they find plenty of food the males make drumming noises on the tree trunks to call other chimps to the feast.

DO YOU KNOW

Chimps are very clever. They use simple tools to get food – as you can see in the picture. Before it can catch termites with a twig, a chimp must cut the twig to the right size and shape.

Some chimps chew leaves to make them spongy – and then use them to soak up water for drinking.

Some chimps have learned to use sticks to crack nuts and get at the juicy kernels inside them.

Chimps often throw sticks and stones at their enemies.

Chimps like to catch and eat tasty termites by poking sticks into their nests.

Adult chimps spend a lot of time grooming their babies and their friends. This helps them to keep their fur and skin clean.

Chimps make simple beds for themselves by weaving thin, leafy branches together. They do not make new beds every night.

 **CHIMP FACTS**

● Chimps live in groups of up to 100 animals. The group leader is usually the noisiest male. Males often quarrel with each other, but female chimps are usually all good friends.

● Male chimps weigh up to 50 kg and are about 170 cm high when they stand up. Female chimps are a bit smaller.

WHICH BIRD HUNTS MONKEYS?

The crowned eagle is the most powerful bird in the African forest. It catches monkeys in the trees and even snatches small antelope from the forest floor. Large wings give it the power to carry animals heavier than itself.

Crowned eagles have to be fast to catch monkeys in the trees. They kill their prey with their huge talons.

DO YOU KNOW

The crowned eagle weighs about 4 kg and is about 75 cm long. It gets its name from the big crest of feathers on its head. Village chiefs once used the feathers in their head-dresses.

WHICH BIRD SEWS A NEST?

The tailor bird makes its nest by sewing leaves together to form a pouch. Using its long beak as a needle, it sews with thin fibres pulled from plants and even with silk from spiders' webs.

TAILOR BIRD FACTS

● Tailor birds are about 12 cm long.

● Tailor birds live in India and other parts of southern Asia. They are often to be found nesting in gardens.

The finished nest is very hard to find in the trees. It is filled with soft fibres. The parents feed the baby birds with caterpillars and other insects.

WHY DO HORNBILLS HAVE BIG BEAKS?

Hornbills live in Africa and Asia. They have enormous beaks, but the beaks are not as heavy as they look. Their long beaks help the birds to reach fruit growing far out on slender twigs. Hornbills nest in tree holes. When a female has settled into a suitable hole, she blocks up the entrance with mud brought by the male. She leaves just enough room to push her beak out. She stays locked up until her eggs hatch. Her mate brings food to her several times a day.

There are 45 different kinds of hornbill. They vary in size from 40 cm to over 120 cm. This one is a Great Indian hornbill.

WHICH ANTS ARE HOMELESS?

Africa's army ants hunt in long columns. They swarm over any animal in their path and tear it to pieces with their jaws. They have no permanent homes. When they have eaten everything around them they march off to camp in another area of the forest.

DO YOU KNOW

Some Africans use the soldier ants to mend wounds. They make the ants bite into the skin on each side of a cut and then snip off the ants' heads. The jaws stay closed and hold the skin together until the wound heals.

Millions of small worker ants march in the column. Each one will carry bits of food back to the camp.

Large soldier ants march beside the column and defend it with their great jaws.

HOW DO WEAVER ANTS MAKE THEIR NESTS?

Weaver ants make bag-like nests with living leaves. One group of ants hold the leaves in place with their jaws and feet and other ants run between them with grubs, or baby ants, in their jaws. The grubs produce sticky silk threads which glue the leaves together.

Weaver ants live in trees and bushes and eat other insects. They kill them with their large jaws or by spraying them with poison.

WHICH ANTS ARE FARMERS?

South America's leaf-cutter ants are the farmers of the ant world. They grow all their own food. Worker ants climb the forest trees and cut small pieces from the leaves. They carry the pieces back to their underground nests, where other workers cut them into smaller pieces and spread them out in special 'gardens'. The leaves soon go mouldy and the ants harvest the mould and eat it. They even manure the gardens with their own droppings to make sure they get good crops.

DO YOU KNOW

Leaf-cutters are also called parasol ants because they carry leaves home over their heads like parasols, or sunshades.

Leaf-cutter ants have big-toothed jaws to slice through the leaves like scissors.

Jaws

Worker ants bring thousands of leaf fragments back to the nest every night, holding them firmly in their jaws.

The workers may travel over 100 metres to cut their leaves. Larger ants called soldiers guard the workers' route.

LEAF-CUTTER FACTS

● Leaf-cutter ants live on farms and in gardens as well as in forests. They destroy all kinds of crops, usually stripping every leaf from a plant before moving on.

WHICH MONKEYS HOWL AND BARK?

Howler monkeys are some of the noisiest animals in the forest. They live in groups and every morning when they wake up they start to howl and bark. These noisy choruses tell other groups of howlers that the area is occupied and warn them to keep away. The monkeys can then feed in peace. They howl again as they settle down for the night.

Howler monkeys live in groups of up to 30 animals. They stay close together as they search for food in the tree-tops.

DO YOU KNOW

Like most other South American monkeys, the howler can wrap its tail round branches and use it like an extra arm or leg as it swings through the trees. African and Asian monkeys cannot do this.

The howler's loud voice comes from its large throat pouch. Males have bigger pouches and louder voices than females.

 HOWLER FACTS

● The howler's voice can carry for about 5 km through the forest.

● Howler monkeys are coloured black or brownish red.

● Their favourite food is wild figs.

18

WHY DO CHAMELEONS STICK OUT THEIR TONGUES?

Chameleons are slow-moving lizards that live in the trees. Lots of different kinds live in the forests of Africa. Although a chameleon moves very slowly, it is very good at catching insects. It traps them with its long, sticky tongue which it shoots out at very high speed. The chameleon has an excellent aim and rarely misses its target.

The chameleon has a very flexible tail and can wrap it round twigs for extra support and safety.

Chameleon eyes can turn in any direction. The animal can even look forwards with one eye and backwards with the other.

? DO YOU KNOW

Chameleons are very good at changing their colours and patterns to match different backgrounds. This helps them to hide from their prey, and also from the snakes and birds that like to eat them.

Long clawed toes give the chameleon a good grip. It rarely moves more than one of its feet at a time.

The chameleon's tongue may be longer than its body. The tongue takes a fraction of a second to shoot out and back again.

WHY DO LEOPARDS HIDE IN TREES?

The leopard is a powerful cat that lives in many parts of Africa and southern Asia. It likes open, rocky country as well as the forests and it is a wonderful climber of both rocks and trees. Leopards usually live alone and feed by night and day. Their prey includes pigs, antelope, monkeys, dogs, and many other animals. A favourite trick is to lie on a branch and drop on to passing prey.

A leopard often uses its great strength to drag the bodies of its victims high into trees, where the meat will be safe from hyaenas and other scavengers.

The spotted coat makes the leopard hard to see in the patchwork of light and shade among the forest trees.

DO YOU KNOW

No two leopards have exactly the same coat pattern. In the wettest areas, a leopard's fur is often completely black. These black leopards are also commonly known as black panthers.

WHERE DOES THE JAGUAR LIVE?

The jaguar is the leopard's powerful American cousin. It lives mainly in the dense forests of South and Central America, usually close to water. It is an excellent swimmer and climber. Jaguars feed mainly on wild pigs and large rodents. They also sprawl by the water and scoop up fish with their huge paws. They even catch alligators and turtles.

Like the leopard, the jaguar is well camouflaged when stalking through the light and shade of the forest.

SURVIVAL WATCH

Jaguars and other spotted cats have long been hunted for their fur. Many jaguars have also been killed because they attack farm animals such as sheep. Jaguars have disappeared from many farming areas, but they are not yet in danger of total extinction as they are found over a huge area – from Mexico to Chile and Argentina.

Jaguar spots form rings like those of the leopard, but a jaguar's rings are different – they nearly all have a spot in the middle.

JAGUAR FACTS

● Jaguars are about as long as leopards, but much fatter. They weigh up to 150 kg.

● A female jaguar has up to four cubs at a time. They stay with her for two years.

WHICH BIRDS HAVE 'PILLOW FIGHTS'?

Toucans have some of the world's biggest beaks. Their beaks are sometimes longer than the rest of the body. These birds live in small flocks and their colourful beaks are used like flags for signalling to each other. Toucans also make loud drumming noises by hitting branches with their beaks. They even have friendly 'pillow fights', in which they whack each other with their beaks until one bird falls off the branch.

Toucans feed mainly on fruit. They also eat frogs and insects, and even steal eggs and chicks from the nests of other birds.

? DO YOU KNOW

Toucans live in South and Central America. They look quite like the hornbills of Africa and Asia (see page 15), but the two families of birds are not related. They look alike because they live in a very similar way, hopping about from branch to branch to gather food.

Hornbill

TOUCAN FACTS

• There are about 40 kinds of toucans.

• Males have longer beaks than females.

• Toucans nest in holes in trees.

The large beak is really very light. Inside it is mostly air, with a mesh of tiny bones supporting the outer shell.

WHICH BIRD IS AN EXCELLENT NUTCRACKER?

Macaws are the world's largest parrots. There are several different kinds and they all live in South America. The macaw is one of the world's best nutcrackers. Its hooked beak can open a Brazil nut with ease – and it can cut off a finger just as easily! The bird first uses the edge of its beak like a saw to cut part way through the shell. Opening the nut is then simple. The macaw also uses its beak as an extra foot when climbing.

The top and bottom parts of the macaw's beak rub against each other and keep the edges sharp.

Two of the toes face forwards and two face backwards. This makes it easy for the macaw to pick things up and grip them.

SURVIVAL WATCH

Macaws are becoming rare because their forest home is being destroyed. They are also caught and sold as pets – macaws are very good at imitating humans, and can learn lots of words, even though they don't know what they mean. Some South American Indians use macaw feathers for decoration.

WHERE DOES THE BEAUTIFUL OCELOT LIVE?

The ocelot is a beautiful cat about 120 cm long, including its tail. It lives in the forests of South and Central America and is a superb climber.

SURVIVAL WATCH

Thousands of ocelots used to be killed every year to make fur coats. Selling the skins is now against the law, but the ocelot is still in danger from the destruction of the forests.

WHERE DO KINKAJOUS LIVE?

The kinkajou looks like a monkey, especially when hanging from its long tail. It lives in the forests of Central and South America. It is a good climber, but does not leap from tree to tree like monkeys.

KINKAJOU FACTS

● The kinkajou's body is about 35 cm long and its tail adds another 45 cm.

● It is more closely related to bears than to monkeys.

WHICH ANIMAL LIVES UPSIDE DOWN?

The sloth does nearly everything upside down. It spends almost all its life hanging upside down in the trees of South and Central America. One of the slowest of all mammals, it may spend its whole life in a single tree. It feeds on leaves and fruits. When a sloth comes down to the ground it cannot walk, but drags itself along with its long claws.

SLOTH FACTS

● Sloths are between 50 and 100 cm long.

● Their top speed through the branches is 1 km/h. It is even less on the ground!

Sloths hang from huge hook-like claws. There are several kinds of sloths, some with only two claws on the front feet.

Tiny plants called algae grow in the sloth's fur and make it go green. Caterpillars also live there and feed on the algae.

The sloth has one baby at a time. The baby clings tightly to its mother for several weeks.

The fur of mammals normally runs from the back to the belly. Sloth fur lies in the other direction so that rain runs off easily.

HOW DO HUMMINGBIRDS HUM?

Hummingbirds are brilliantly coloured birds, named for the humming noise they make with their rapidly beating wings. They dart quickly from place to place and can even hover and fly backwards. There are over 300 species, all living in North, Central and South America. Hummingbirds feed on nectar and insects. They use up so much energy in flight that they have to eat more than their own weight of food every day.

 **DO YOU KNOW**

Some hummingbirds fly off to new areas when the seasons change. The ruby-throated hummingbird flies non-stop across the Gulf of Mexico in a time of about 20 hours. The birds get their energy from fat stored in their bodies before they leave.

THE SWORDBILL

The body of the sword-bill hummingbird is only about 7 cm long, but it has a sword-like beak up to 12 cm long. It can also poke its slender tongue out another 5 or 6 cm. With this amazing equipment, the bird can get nectar from really deep bell-shaped or tubular flowers.

When a hummingbird is hovering, its wings whirr round like tiny propellers. They beat up to 100 times every second and this is what produces the humming noise.

Hummingbirds suck sugary nectar from flowers while they are hovering. They also catch small insects and spiders.

Hummingbirds make their nests with spider silk and pieces of bark or lichen. Hovering parents feed their chicks by pumping nectar and insects into their gaping beaks.

HUMMINGBIRD FACTS

● The biggest species of hummingbird is only 20 cm long.

● The smallest type is the bee hummingbird of Cuba. It is under 6 cm long, including its beak and tail. It is the smallest of all birds.

● Some hummingbirds can fly at 100 km/h over short distances.

WHICH IS THE BIGGEST CAT?

The tiger is the largest member of the cat family. It lives in the forests of Asia, and also by rivers where there is plenty of tall grass in which it can hide. The tiger is not a fast runner and, like most cats, it stalks silently towards its prey. When it is near enough it leaps out and knocks its prey down with one swipe of a great paw. Deer, pigs, and antelope are the tiger's main prey. It usually hunts alone and at night.

The tiger uses its large dagger-like teeth to stab its prey. One bite in the throat or the back of the neck is enough to kill a deer.

SURVIVAL WATCH

Many tigers have been shot for their beautiful fur, or because they have killed farm animals. Much of the tiger's forest home has also been destroyed to make way for farms, so the animal is now in real danger. There may be only a few hundred tigers left.

DO YOU KNOW

Tigers don't like to get too hot. They spend really hot days lying in pools and streams.

The tiger's roar can be heard over 2 km away. It roars to defend its territory or to call its mate or cubs.

The tiger's striped coat camouflages it very well as it stalks through the grass. Its unsuspecting prey is taken completely by surprise.

WHICH BAT LOOKS LIKE A FOX?

The flying fox is a big fruit-eating bat with a face like that of a fox. Several kinds live in tropical Asia and Australia. They live in big flocks, eating valuable fruit crops and damaging trees.

The bat's wing is made of flexible skin stretched over its very long fingers. The wings span nearly 2 metres, but the bat weighs only 1 kg.

HOW DO GLIDING FROGS GLIDE?

Gliding frogs live high in the forest trees of South-East Asia. Flaps of skin between their toes act like parachutes, helping the frogs to glide gently from one tree to the next as they search for insects to eat.

Gliding frogs even lay their eggs in the trees. They lay them in packets of foam wrapped in leaves. When the eggs hatch, the tiny tadpoles drop down to live in pools on the ground.

Sticky pads on the gliding frog's toes help it to climb. Using these pads, it can cling to even the smoothest of leaves.

WHO IS THE OLD MAN OF THE WOODS?

Orang-utans live only on the islands of Borneo and Sumatra in South-East Asia. Their name means 'old man of the woods', which makes sense because old males often grow beards and look quite like old men. Orang-utans spend most of their time in the trees and, although they are slower than the gibbons, they are amazing climbers.

The orang's legs are not as strong as its arms, but its long toes are very good at gripping the branches while it climbs.

Like the other apes, the orang has no tail. It has long red hair, but it is not as hairy all over as most of the other apes.

 SURVIVAL WATCH

The orang-utan is very rare because its forest home is being rapidly destroyed. Orangs are also caught and sold as pets. Special reserves have been set up so that the remaining few animals can live there in safety.

HOW ARE GIBBONS SUITED TO THE HIGH LIFE?

Gibbons are built for life high in the trees. They move through the tree-tops at high speed, usually by swinging hand over hand along the branches. Their powerful arms are actually longer than their legs. Gibbons live in family groups and make a lot of noise to let other groups know where they are. They feed mainly on fruit.

Gibbons often leap from tree to tree. Long, strong fingers give them a secure grip on the branches.

 GIBBON FACTS

● There are several different kinds of gibbons and they all live in South-East Asia.

● Gibbons look like monkeys, but they have no tails and they are really small apes.

Gibbons have no nests, so the baby has to go wherever its mother goes. It clings tightly to her as she swings through the branches.

The gibbon has a wonderful sense of balance. It uses its arms to steady itself as it walks along thin branches.

WHY DO PEACOCKS FAN THEIR TAILS?

The peacock has some of the world's biggest feathers. He spreads them into a magnificent fan when he sees a female. If she likes the display she will become his mate. Peacocks eat almost anything, from seeds to mice and snakes. Although they feed on the ground, they sleep in the trees at night. They often live around villages.

While displaying, the peacock shakes his feathers from time to time and produces a loud rattling noise.

PEACOCK FACTS

● Peacocks live in India and Sri Lanka.

● Males are over 250 cm long, including the train of feathers.

● Peacocks are very noisy birds, with piercing screams.

Some of the feathers are over 1 metre long. When he is not displaying, the bird folds his fan up and drags it behind him.

The female is called a peahen. She is less colourful than the male. She lays up to 20 eggs in a nest on the ground.

WHICH BIRDS DANCE UPSIDE DOWN?

The birds of paradise have some of the most beautiful feathers in the world. The males show off their long, colourful plumes when they dance to attract the females. Many of the dances are performed while hanging upside down like trapeze artistes. Birds of paradise live in the forests of New Guinea and Northern Australia. The one shown here is the red-plumed bird of paradise.

2. He then flutters his wings and bends forward. At the end of his dance he is hanging upside down from the branch.

1. The male begins his courtship dance by lifting his wings and spreading out his beautiful red plumes.

 SURVIVAL WATCH

Birds of paradise used to be killed so their feathers could be used on ladies' hats. Today the feathers are still used for head-dresses.

The females are rather dull birds. They choose their mates after watching the males' displays.

HOW DID BIRDWINGS GET THEIR NAME?

Birdwings got their name because they seem more like birds than butterflies when they flap past your head. They include some of the world's biggest and most beautiful butterflies. They live in the forests of South-East Asia, New Guinea and northern Australia. Many species have become rare because butterfly collectors have caught so many. The destruction of their forest homes is making them even rarer.

This is Rajah Brooke's birdwing, from Malaysia and Indonesia. Thousands are caught every year, but this species is still quite common in some areas.

DO YOU KNOW

Female birdwings usually stay high in the trees. Many of them are dull brown, but female Rajah Brooke's birdwings are nearly as bright as the males.

BIRDWING FACTS

● The largest species is Queen Alexandra's birdwing, with wings over 25 cm across.

● The wings of many species are used to make jewellery.

The wing colours often change as you move round and look at the wings from different angles.

WHICH FROGS ARE DEADLY POISONOUS?

Arrow-poison frogs are among the most poisonous animals on Earth. The poison is in the skin. The frogs got their name because the South American Indians use them to poison the tips of their hunting arrows. A tiny scratch from a poisoned arrow can kill a large animal such as a jaguar. Animals killed by the arrows are safe to eat because the poison is destroyed when it is swallowed.

 **DO YOU KNOW**

The male carries the eggs and tadpoles on his back. The tadpoles feed on food stored in the eggs. When the food has gone the male sets the tadpoles free in some water.

POISON FROG FACTS

● Some arrow-poison frogs are so poisonous that one gram of poison is enough to kill 100,000 people.

● Some species are under 2 cm long.

Arrow-poison frogs have brilliant colours, warning other rain forest animals that they are poisonous and should be left alone.

Most arrow-poison frogs have suction pads on their toes, helping them to cling safely to wet and shiny leaves.

Asiatic elephants are the biggest animals in the forests of Asia, although they are not quite as big as their African cousins. The females and youngsters roam about in small herds. Older males join them in the breeding season and sometimes have terrible fights with their tusks. Many elephants have been trained to work in the forests, where they are much better than machines for getting between the trees to pull out big logs.

The elephant's tusks are very large teeth. They are made of ivory. Females usually have smaller tusks than males.

The elephant loves bathing and drinks up to 200 litres of water in a day. It squirts the water into its mouth with its flexible trunk.

The Asiatic elephant has a strongly arched back, quite unlike the rather flat back of the African elephant.

ELEPHANT FACTS

• The Asiatic elephant is often called the Indian elephant.

• It has a domed forehead and a smoother trunk than the African elephant, and its tusks are usually shorter. It weighs up to 6 tonnes.

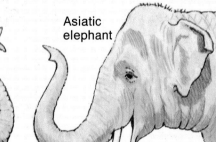

African elephant

Asiatic elephant

An elephant can drag huge logs from the forest and pick them up with its trunk and tusks. Each elephant has its own rider.

SURVIVAL WATCH

Asiatic elephants are not in as much danger as African elephants, but they are much less common than they were 100 years ago. The forests in which they live are gradually being destroyed, and the odd thing about this is that the tamed, working elephants are helping to cause the damage. Large areas of forest must be preserved in order to protect Asia's wild elephants.

Elephants feed almost entirely on leaves, which they pull from the trees and shove into their mouths with their trunks.

The ears do not reach down as far as the mouth. They are much smaller than the ears of an African elephant.

WHY ARE RAIN FORESTS IN DANGER?

Rain forests are among the most threatened places on Earth. Millions of trees are cut down each year for timber. Huge areas are also felled every day to make way for farming. Thousands of animals are probably becoming extinct every year because there is nowhere left for them to live. Even if new trees are planted, these places will never get their original wildlife back again.

Many kinds of beautiful forest birds and insects will never be seen again because their forest homes are being cut down. The problem is especially bad in South America and South-East Asia.

 GREENHOUSE EFFECT

Every time we breathe, we give out a gas called carbon dioxide. The same gas is made in car engines and whenever we burn anything. It forms a layer round the Earth and traps heat, just like greenhouse glass. The heat warms the Earth and can cause droughts and other big changes in the world's weather. Trees use up carbon dioxide, so cutting down the rain forests is making this 'Greenhouse Effect' even worse.

USEFUL WORDS

Algae   A group of simple plants that usually live in water and damp places. Many of them are very small.

Ape   Any of the large, monkey-like animals that are our own closest relatives in the animal world. Gorillas, chimpanzees, orang-utans, and gibbons are all apes. They differ from monkeys in having no tails.

Camouflage   The way in which animals avoid the attention of their enemies by resembling their surroundings or blending in with them. The animals are then not easy to see.

Courtship   The process of attracting a mate. Animals often do this by showing off their bright colours.

Equator   The imaginary line running around the centre of the Earth. This divides the Earth into two halves, called the northern and southern hemispheres.

Evergreen   A tree or shrub that keeps its leaves throughout the year.

Extinct   An animal is extinct when it no longer exists anywhere in the world. Many kinds of animal are in danger of extinction.

Hover   To remain at one place in the air, without moving forwards or backwards. Hummingbirds hover by beating their wings very rapidly.

Mammal   Any animal that feeds its babies with milk from the mother's body. Mammals live almost everywhere, and there are many kinds in the rain forests, including monkeys, leopards and elephants.

Nature reserve   An area set aside to protect wild plants and animals – often rare ones which are in danger of becoming extinct.

Nectar   The sugary juice produced by flowers. Many insects and birds feed on it.

Nocturnal   Active during the night.

Predator   Any animal that hunts or traps other animals for food. Predators can also be the prey of other animals.

Prey   An animal that is caught and eaten by a predator.

Scavenger   An animal that feeds mainly on dead matter – especially one that clears up the remains left behind from another animal's meal.

Species   A species is any one particular kind of animal or plant, such as a tiger or an ocelot.

Tadpole   The fish-like early stage in the life of a frog or a toad.

Termite   Termites are small ant-like insects that live in large colonies – often in tree trunks or in mounds of soil. They are common in most tropical areas and are eaten by all sorts of other creatures.

Territory   The area in which an animal or group of animals live. Animals defend their territory against other animals of the same kind.

Tropical   To do with the tropics. These are warm areas of the world, on either side of the Equator.

INDEX